THE CANADIAN
ROCKIES
THROUGH THE SEASONS

The mountains, glaciers and valleys of the Canadian Rockies are
constantly changing. However, the seasons reflect a more visual change to the
scenery. Landscape photogragher Graeme Wallace has been capturing the changing
moods of the Canadian Rocky Mountains for many years, often returning
to the same place time after time. He has spent seven years working on this book and
hopes that it will give you an insight into how this spectacular mountain
region changes across the seasons.

PHOTOGRAPHY BY GRAEME WALLACE

published by GW Publishing

INTRODUCTION

A region of magnificent vistas, vivid turquoise lakes, mighty waterfalls, rugged glacier capped peaks and emerald waters are just some of the phrases which have been used to describe the Canadian Rocky Mountains. Ever since the earliest visitors to the Rockies struggled to find words to describe what they had seen, writers and photographers still fail to fully prepare new visitors for the parks' stunning scenery. Only after visiting the region can you begin to comprehend its magnificent beauty.

Perhaps the greatest claim the Canadian Rockies can make is its achievement as a World Heritage Site in 1985 for the four national parks of Banff, Jasper, Yoho and Kootenay, followed by Mt Robson and Mt Assiniboine provincial parks in 1990.

Most visitors come in the Summer, but each season has its unique mood and colors and we hope this book has captured those seasonal variations.

Spring in the Canadian Rockies starts in late March and continues through to mid June. Although there is still snow on the ground in March and April, it quickly thaws in May leaving only the higher mountain trails covered by June. Many of the lakes remain ice covered until mid May, with some of the higher lakes, including Moraine Lake and Bow Lake, partially frozen until mid June. The waterfalls are heavy with melt-water from the snow, although the glaciers do not start to melt until late Spring. The lakes appear most vibrant in the brief period between their thaw and the time the glaciers begin to melt.

Summer generally occurs between mid June and mid August. However, even at this time of year, particularly August, snowfall may occur on the peaks of some mountains. The majority of plants are blooming throughout this season.

The glacier lakes are heavy with silt from the melting glaciers resulting in a cloudy appearance in early Summer. The lakes become a clearer more vivid turquoise color as the Summer progresses.

Autumn season starts in mid August and rapidly sets in through September and October. The temperature drops quite rapidly and freezing often occurs during the night This is the season when the valleys and mountain sides become alive in a vast array of reds, golds and greens. The last two weeks of September are generally the best to see the needles of the Lyall's Larch tree turn golden, while the Aspen's leaves turn yellow in mid October. Elk are now rutting and move out into the open to fight for dominance, paying little attention to humans passing by. By November some of the smaller lakes have already frozen over.

Winter returns in November, depositing a blanket of snow through to late March. The heaviest snow stays away until December when the temperature drops to -40°C and a wind chill off the prairies makes it feel even colder in the valleys. All the lakes freeze over, as do the rivers, and although they may appear dormant above ground, the fish are still very much alive in the icy water. The water level in the rivers drops considerably often leaving a gap of several feet between its surface and the frozen ice. Waterfalls also freeze resulting in shear walls of ice. The weather remains cold and clear until mid February when it starts to warm and bring a little more snow.

While pictures and words cannot completely describe the scenery of the Rockies we hope this book will give you the opportunity to see how this mountain region changes through the year and will encourage you to return in a different season.

ACKNOWLEDGEMENTS

Photography by **Graeme Wallace**

Edited by **Virginia Smith**

Designed by **Samantha Williams**

Reprographics by **LC Repro**

Printed by **Trento**

Published by

GW Publishing

Calleva Business Park

Aldermaston

Reading

Great Britain

Tel 01144 1189 821110

First Published in 1999

Revised in 2000

ISBN 0 9535397 0 9

Goods Clasification Number 4901-9900

To order prints of pictures in this book, visit our Web site at

www.gwpublishing.com

In an attempt to focus on the natural grandeur of the Canadian Rockies this book is
presented in a clean and simple style, incorporating many full page spreads
of powerful panoramic images. The maps on pages 8 and 9 include the page number of
each photograph for easy reference. Man-made developments are essential to
cater for the large number of people visiting the parks, and just as these developments
have been restricted in the parks, we have endeavoured to restrict the number
of pictures reflecting human influence in the parks. Views of Banff and Jasper towns have
been included to illustrate how well they merge into their surroundings.
However, we must not forget that if it were not for the hundreds of people who work in
the parks, our visit would not have been so comfortable or informative.

Pictured above and on the previous page, the road along the world famous Icefield Parkway takes
you over two mountain passes to within easy access of some of the most stunning scenery in
the Rockies. The highlight along the Parkway must be the Athabasca Glacier situated halfway
along the 230 kilometer road on the Banff / Jasper boundary.

CONTENTS

BANFF, KOOTENAY, ASSINIBOINE AND YOHO PARKS

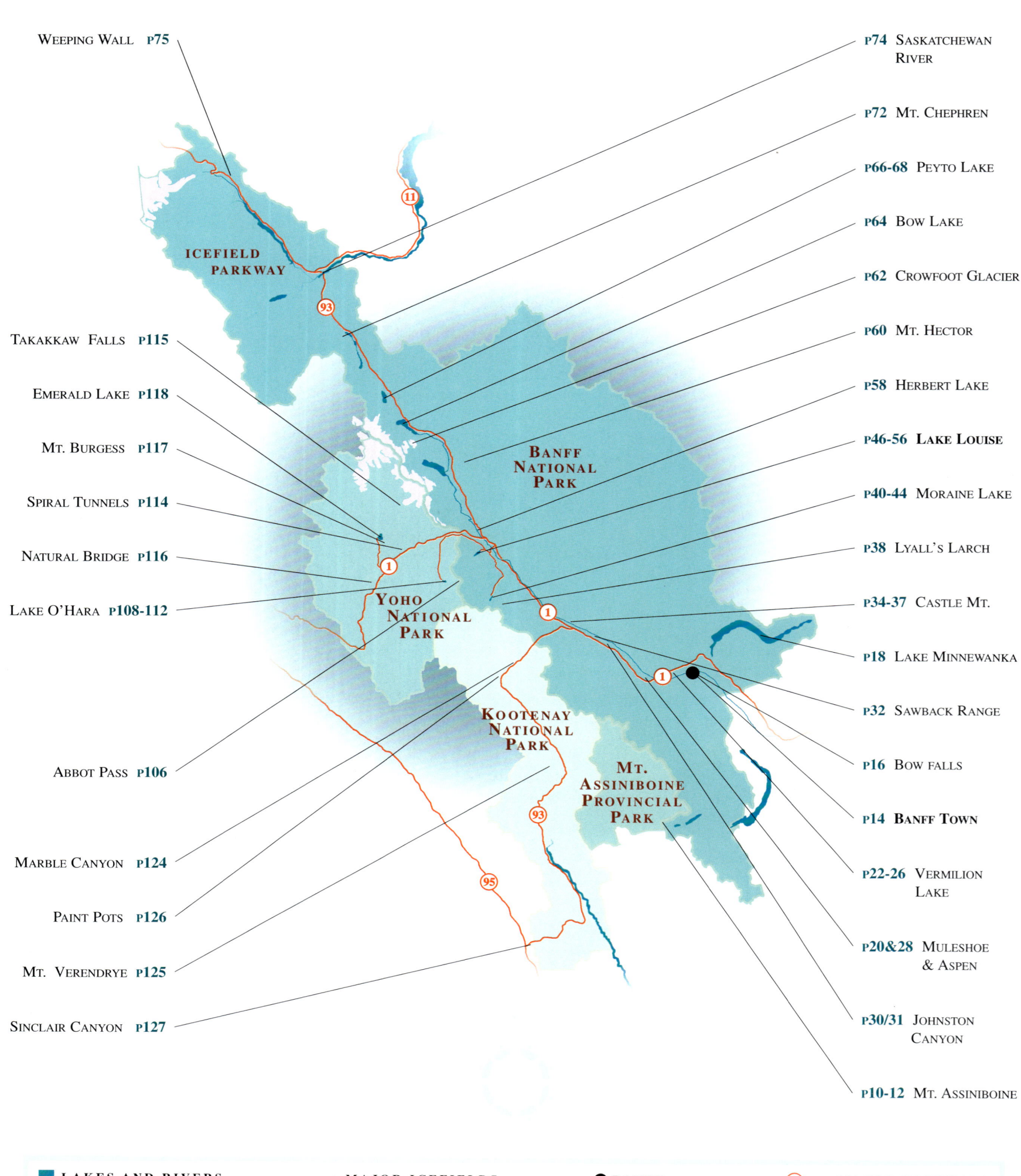

WEEPING WALL **P75**

P74 SASKATCHEWAN RIVER

P72 MT. CHEPHREN

P66-68 PEYTO LAKE

P64 BOW LAKE

P62 CROWFOOT GLACIER

P60 MT. HECTOR

P58 HERBERT LAKE

P46-56 **LAKE LOUISE**

P40-44 MORAINE LAKE

P38 LYALL'S LARCH

P34-37 CASTLE MT.

P18 LAKE MINNEWANKA

P32 SAWBACK RANGE

P16 BOW FALLS

P14 **BANFF TOWN**

P22-26 VERMILION LAKE

P20&28 MULESHOE & ASPEN

P30/31 JOHNSTON CANYON

P10-12 MT. ASSINIBOINE

TAKAKKAW FALLS **P115**

EMERALD LAKE **P118**

MT. BURGESS **P117**

SPIRAL TUNNELS **P114**

NATURAL BRIDGE **P116**

LAKE O'HARA **P108-112**

ABBOT PASS **P106**

MARBLE CANYON **P124**

PAINT POTS **P126**

MT. VERENDRYE **P125**

SINCLAIR CANYON **P127**

ICEFIELD PARKWAY

BANFF NATIONAL PARK

YOHO NATIONAL PARK

KOOTENAY NATIONAL PARK

MT. ASSINIBOINE PROVINCIAL PARK

■ LAKES AND RIVERS   MAJOR ICEFIELDS   ● BANFF   ○— MAJOR HIGHWAYS

8

JASPER AND MOUNT ROBSON PARKS

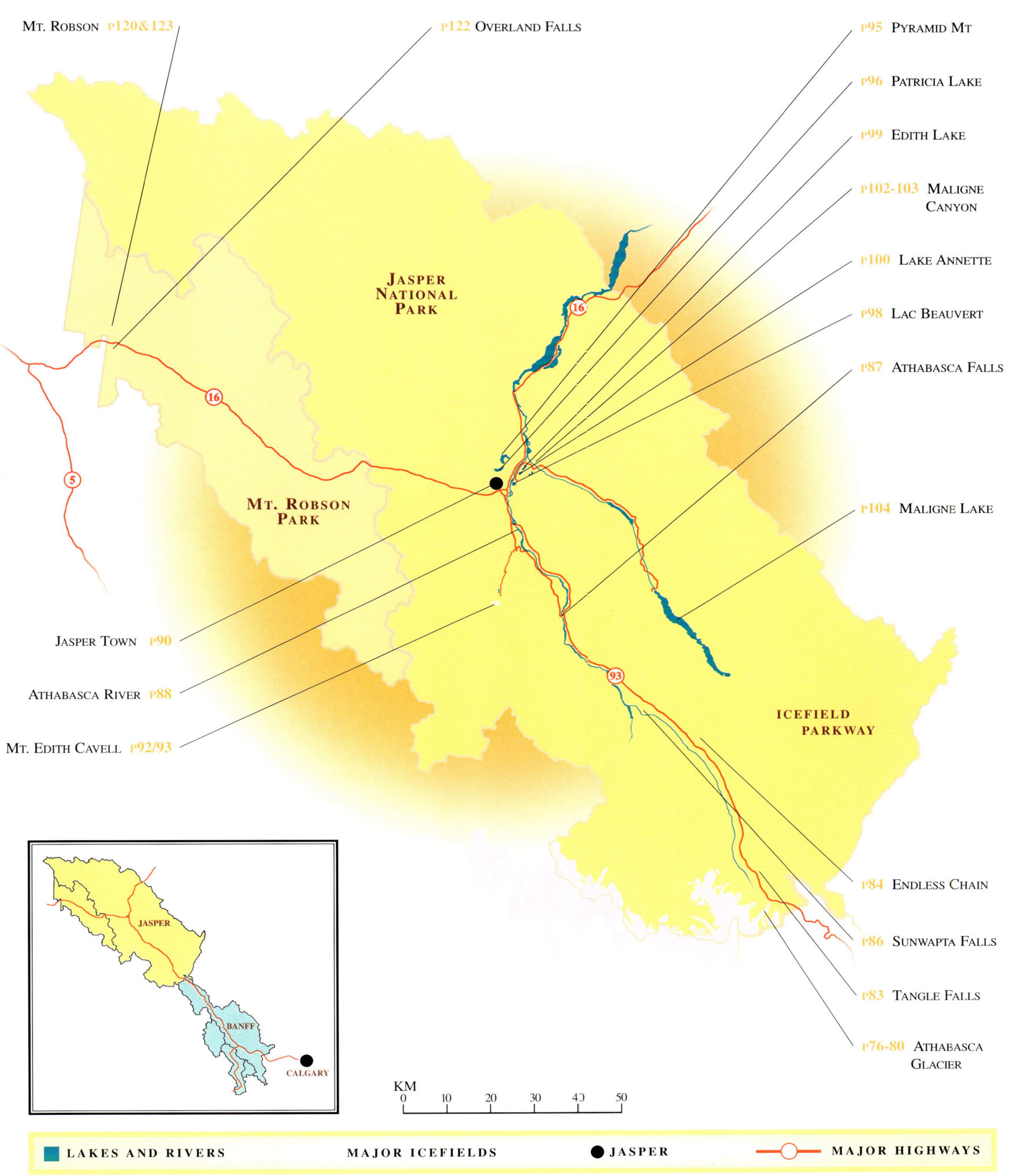

MT. ROBSON P120&123

P122 OVERLAND FALLS

JASPER
NATIONAL
PARK

MT. ROBSON
PARK

P95 PYRAMID MT

P96 PATRICIA LAKE

P99 EDITH LAKE

P102-103 MALIGNE
CANYON

P100 LAKE ANNETTE

P98 LAC BEAUVERT

P87 ATHABASCA FALLS

P104 MALIGNE LAKE

JASPER TOWN P90

ATHABASCA RIVER P88

MT. EDITH CAVELL P92/93

ICEFIELD
PARKWAY

P84 ENDLESS CHAIN

P86 SUNWAPTA FALLS

P83 TANGLE FALLS

P76-80 ATHABASCA
GLACIER

JASPER

BANFF

CALGARY

KM
0   10   20   30   40   50

LAKES AND RIVERS   MAJOR ICEFIELDS   ●JASPER   ──○── MAJOR HIGHWAYS

9

MT ASSINIBOINE PROVINCIAL PARK

Mt Assiniboine *(Opposite) Named after the native Assiniboine Tribe.*

Mount Assiniboine Provincial Park is situated South of Banff National Park
on the Alberta, BC boundary. 3618 m Mt. Assiniboine, called the 'Canadian Matterhorn,'
is the principal mountain in the park and although it may appear to be the highest
mountain in the Canadian Rockies, there are five other mountains which stand taller.
Named after the native Assiniboine Tribe, the breath-taking area around
the mountain is only accessible by horseback, a two day hike or by helicopter.

Coyote *(Above) A little smaller than the wolf, coyotes are less reclusive and are
common throughout the parks. Although surrounded by Autumn colors the coyote above, like
all coyotes is colorblind.*

Mt Assiniboine *(Following page) is unmistakable as the morning
sunrise catches its peak through the clouds.*

BANFF NATIONAL PARK

Banff Ave. (*Above*)

Banff National Park, formerly called Rocky Mountains
National Park, was established in 1887 as
Canada's first national park. The Canadian Pacific
Railway was instrumental in establishing the
park which has grown to encompass 6641 sq. km.
With Cascade Mountain situated at the head of
the high street, and the Bow River flowing through the
town, Banff has been a major base for tourists
heading into the Rocky Mountains from both the south
and the Canadian Pacific railroad.
During the winter the town becomes a refuge not only
for skiers but also for elk, which move into the town
to eat any greenery still exposed.

Banff Town (*Opposite*) *The Sulphur Mountain Gondola
provides an excellent opportunity to survey
the town and the surrounding lakes and mountains.*

Cave and Basin Hot Springs (*Above*) *Discovered in 1875, the 33°C sulphur rich waters attracted many early visitors believing in its healing properties, and led to the establishment of Banff Town and National Park.*

Bow Falls (*Opposite*) *Flowing south from Bow Lake along the Icefield Parkway and the Bow Valley Parkway, the relentless Bow River thunders over the limestone bedrock of Bow Falls as it meanders through the town of Banff on its way to Calgary. The falls are at their most powerful during the Spring months.*

Lake Miniwanka (*Opposite*) known as the "Lake of the
Water Spirit," has been dammed twice, once in 1912
and again in 1941, raising the lake by
24 meters and making it the largest lake in Banff Park.
Since then nature has been active in
altering and reshaping the landscape around the lake.

Fireweeds *(Following page) cover the ground of an
Aspen forest floor along the Bow Valley Highway, setting
it alight in shades of brilliant red during the Autumn.*

Viewed from the lush mountain wetlands of the Vermilion Lakes, the serated knife edge of Mount Rundle reaches a height of 2,999m west of Banff town. These shallow, tranquil lakes are the habitat of many reclusive species including bald eagles, moose and beaver.

3rd Vermilion Lake (*Opposite*) *These fresh water lakes are also the habitat of trout which attract both fishermen and eagles alike.*

2nd Vermilion Lake (*Following page*) *Unlike the glacier fed lakes in the region, due to their shallow depth, these lakes never totally freeze over or form a thick layer of ice.*

2nd Vermilion Lake (*Opposite*) *The Vermilion Lakes consist of three beaver dammed adjoining lakes connected by marshes on the outskirts of Banff town.*

Muleshoe (*Following page*) *Growing in the marshland of the meandering Bow River, muskeg explodes into vibrant shades of red and orange during the Autumn.*

Johnston Canyon Upper Falls *(Opposite)* A series of catwalks and trails lead along the cliffside of the Canyon to a total of seven waterfalls. The water drops a clear 30 meters over the upper falls, while a bridge provides very close access to the base of the lower falls.

Johnston Canyon *(Above)* One of the smaller falls along Johnston Canyon.

The Bow Valley Parkway, between Banff and Lake Louise, runs parallel to the Trans-Canada Highway but at a slower pace. This alternative route provides an excellent opportunity to see wildlife, together with a great deal of colorful scenery all year round.

Sawback Range *(Following page)* The new Spring growth of trembling Aspen contrasting with the snow covered peaks of the Sawback Mountain Range announces that Spring has once again arrived.

Castle Mt *(Previous page)* *Rising 2,766 m high like an imposing medieval fortress mid-way between Banff and Lake Louise along the Bow River, Castle Mountain is a classic example of the castellated or layered mountains that characterise the Eastern main ranges. The horizontally layered soft sedimentary and quartzite rock is unable to withstand the erosion from the harsh weather just as it was unable to withstand the erosion of glacial ice thousands of years ago.*

Castle Mt *(Below)* *A close-up view reveals the sculptured ridge of the mountain face.*

Bow River *(Opposite)* *A stag guides his herd of elk across the Bow River under a moonlit Summer sky.*

Lyall's Larch Trees *(Following page)* *A deciduous conifer tree which only grows in the upper subalpine forest. Found near high altitude lakes, such as Moraine Lake, their needles turn golden yellow in Autumn before they are shed.*

Moraine Lake (*Previous page*) *Moraine Lake is arguably the most stunning lake in the Rockies. The vivid turquoise water surrounded by the white-capped Ten Peaks of the Wenkchemna Mountain Range provides a tranquil yet rugged location. A large rock pile at the foot of the lake provides an excellent elevation to look down on the lake and from here the water appears even more colorful.*
Moraine Lake was first seen by a white man in 1894, 12 years after Lake Louise was seen and yet it is only 20 km away. Samuel Allan referred to the lake as being a "grand but gloomy and dark lake" and named the lake Heejee. (One can only assume he first saw the lake on an overcast day). The lake was later renamed Moraine Lake by his friend Walter Wilcox.

Moraine Lake (*Opposite*) *remains frozen until the beginning of June at which time its vivid turquoise color is revealed.*

Elk (*Above*) *The stags grow new antlers each year and are at their finest during the Autumn rutting season.*

Moraine Lake (*Following page*) *At an elevation of 1887 m, 150 meters higher than Lake Louise, Moraine Lake remains frozen several weeks after Lake Louise has thawed.*

Lake Louise *(Previous page) A classic view of Banff National Park's world famous centrepiece. The water appears cloudy due to the amount of silt and rock flour produced and deposited by Victoria Glacier at the head of the lake.*

Considered by many as the centrepiece of the Canadian Rockies, Lake Louise was first seen by a white person in 1882. Explorer Tom Wilson wrote, "As God is my judge I never in all my explorations....... saw such a matchless scene."

Victoria Glacier *(Above) Although it has receded by over 1,200 meters in 160 years, Victoria Glacier is still 60-91m deep, situated 3464m high on Mt. Victoria, 9km from the shore of Lake Louise.*

Lake Louise *(Opposite) still holds its charm at dawn, as the rising sun tints the glacier ice of Mount Victoria.*

Many lakes in the Rockies appear a turquoise blue. These are glacier lakes, and the
glacier is often clearly visible in the valley at the head of the lake. As the
glacier moves, rocks and debris build up inside and underneath the ice. These rocks,
trapped within the ice, are ground against the mountain side and against
each other producing a fine rock powder known as 'rock flour.' As the glacier ice starts to
melt in late Spring, the melt-water flows, often hundreds of meters, carrying
the muddy silt to the lake as seen in the picture below.
While the heavier debris may never make it to the lake the tiny particles of rock flour
remaining in the melt-water become evenly distributed throughout the lake.
When light hits the water the suspended rock flour reflects, or filters out, all the colors of
the spectrum except the blue/green and turquoise. This becomes
more noticeable when viewed from a higher vantage point and on a sunny day.

Lake Louise (*Above*) *The sandy colored deposit at the head of the lake is not sand, it is the
very fine rock flour particles which give the lake its unique color.*

In the late Spring and Summer large quantities of rock flour are deposited into the lakes which results in the water appearing a milky green. *(See picture opposite.)*
During the Autumn and Winter much of the flour settles to the bottom of the lakes with the remaining evenly distributed particles giving the water an intense blue appearance in the Spring. The colorful water can be seen at its most intense just after the ice covering the lakes melts, and before they once again start to fill with the rock flour. *(See picture above.)*

Lake Louise *(Following page) A thin layer of ice still covers the lake in the late Spring but will have disappeared within a few days.*

Ground squirrel *(Below)* *There are a variety of species of ground squirrel. This, however, is the one most frequently seen by visitors to the Rockies. It has two white lines running along its back and a reddish-brown head. It is easily mistaken for a chipmunk which is slightly smaller and has a striped head. Ground squirrels, like rocky terrain and are very common around Moraine Lake and Lake Louise.*

Lake Agnes *(Opposite)* *is a glacier tarn situated high in the mountains above Lake Louise. Referred to as "The Lake in the Clouds," it is accessible by a short but steep hike from Lake Louise.*

Lake Louise *(Following page)* *At 1731 m (1 mile) above sea level, Lake Louise is 83 m deep and 2.4 km long. Situated in a mountain valley it can expect twice as much snow as the lower Bow Valley. The lake will freeze up to 1 meter deep, thick enough to take the weight of a vehicle, and the various Winter activities which take place on the ice.*

ICEFIELD PARKWAY

Acknowledged as one of the most scenic drives in the world, the Icefield Parkway runs
parallel to the Great Divide. Several icefields span the Great Divide to the West of
the highway which is where this parkway derives its name. Adjoining the Banff and Jasper
National Parks at the Sunwapta pass, the 230 km long parkway from Lake Louise
to Jasper can be travelled in three hours. However, as the next 20 pages portray there is
much to see and a full day or more could easily be taken to really appreciate the glacier
carved mountains and valleys, the intense lakes, mighty waterfalls, abundant wildlife and
the stunning glaciers. To travel the parkway in less than a day is to do it a grave injustice.

Herbert Lake (*Previous page*) *Peaceful Herbert Lake is the first lake visitors
come across driving North up the Icefield Parkway. Unlike many lakes in the Rockies it is not
glacier fed and therefore appears clear and blue rather than cloudy and turquoise.
Although relatively small, in the calm of morning it acts as a
stunning mirror for the distant Bow Mountain Range surrounding Lake Louise.*

Bow Peak (*Above*) *Bow Peak 2868m is one of the dominant mountains forming part of the
Eastern Main Range. These mountains are formed by layers of uplifted sedimentary rock.*

Mount Hector (*Opposite*) *The snow covered peaks become more dramatic
as the sun highlights the ridges and cliffs. Clear blue Winter skies provide a stark contrast
to the rugged white mountains.*

Crowfoot Glacier (*Opposite*) *So called because of its former resemblance to a crow's foot (one of its 'toes' has fallen away) Crowfoot Glacier is a classic example of ice build-up which has overflowed from the huge Wapta Icefield, but which is now rapidly receding. However, it is still much bigger than it appears from across the Bow Lake, being 50 m deep at the visible face.*

Crowfoot Glacier (*Below*) *Even in Winter the blue glacial ice is still evident.*

Bow Lake (*Following page*) *Fed by the receding Bow Glacier, seen in the centre of the photograph, Bow Lake stretches along the Icefield Parkway with Crowfoot Glacier at the far end and is one of the largest bodies of water in the region. Situated 1974 m above sea level this is one of the highest lakes in the Canadian Rockies and is therefore one of the first to freeze and last to thaw.*

Peyto Lake *(Opposite)* *is known as "The bluest lake in the Rockies." Looking down from Bow Summit observation platform 2115m above sea level, Lake Peyto 250m below must be one of the most breathtaking and dramatic sights in the world. Even after having seen some of the other glacier lakes in the area, nothing can prepare you for the sight of the deep turquoise water combined with the magnificent panoramic vista along the Mistaya Valley.*

Indian Paint Brush *(Above)* *is one of the more common montane wild flowers in the Rockies and grows in abundance along the trail to Peyto Lake through mid May to late August.*

Peyto Lake *(Opposite) This area of the Icefield Parkway is very remote. Snow covers the ground up to nine months of the year leaving a very brief Summer period during which the wild flowers bloom.*

Glacier Lily *(Above) An early flowering plant, its bright yellow petals are often seen through the melting snow from mid May to June.*

There are an estimated 200 black bear in the parks, but being less wary of humans, they
are more frequently seen than the grizzly bear.
Two to three feet high when on four legs, they are smaller and rounder then grizzlies and
have a straight muzzle and larger ears.
Hibernating from late October to mid May they gorge themselves
from late Summer before moving up from the montane woodland into the subalpine
forests where they dig a den for the Winter.

Black Bear (*Above*) *Although omnivorous, the black bear's diet is about 75% vegetarian and
it can often be seen along roadsides eating berries and new Spring vegetation. The remainder
of its diet is made up of insects and carrion and a small amount of fish and smaller mammals.*

Black Bears *(Above) Although called the black bear they are not always black in color. The sow above was seen with a pair of one year old cubs, one black the other brown.*

Mt. Chepren *(Following page) One of the highest peaks along the Icefield Parkway, Mt. Chepren at the foot of the Waterfowl Lakes stands dominant and proud.*

Sask River Cross *(Below) The main source of the Saskatchewan River is the Saskatchewan Glacier. However, it is joined by water from many other rivers and glaciers before diverting at the Saskatchewan River Crossing and flowing hundreds of kilometers across 3 provinces of Canada to the Hudson Bay.*

Weeping Wall *(Opposite) Water permeating through cracks in Cirrus Mountain forms the Weeping Wall. A wall of blue ice during the Winter, it appears to be "weeping" heaviest in June.*

Athabasca Glacier *(Previous page)* *When viewed in comparison to smaller neighbouring*
glaciers such as Dome and Stutfield Glacier, the 6 km long and 1 km wide
Athabasca Glacier appears huge. However, it only represents a relatively small overflow of the
325 sq km Columbia Icefield which lies just over the ridge. The Icefield is the
largest south of the Arctic Circle and is up to 250 m deep.
The Athabasca Glacier once spilled out across the road along the Icefield Parkway but has
retreated considerably in the last 100 years. Due to the high elevation and cold temperatures of
the Canadian Rockies, the heavy snow fall exceeds the amount of snow melt. The remaining
snow eventually becomes glacier ice, but not at a rate to prevent the glaciers from retreating.

Athabasca Glacier *(Opposite)* A closer inspection of the glacier toe
reveals undulating surfaces and deep hazardous crevasses where the glacier has repeatedly
thawed and refrozen over the years.

(Above) Hardy vegetation still grows in the alpine region and has adapted
well to the severe conditions.

Athabasca Glacier *(Following page)* *Specially adapted snow coaches provide visitors with the*
unique opportunity to stand on top of the glacier.

Mountain Goat *(Below) The steep rocky terrain along the Icefield Parkway provides a safe environment for the mountain goat. During the Spring they often come down from the safety of the mountain sides to lick the minerals from the roads. When their thick Winter coats moult in June, they look more like an antelope to which they are closely related.*

Tangle Falls *(Opposite) Melt water from the thawing snow streams over the steep cliff sides of Tangle Ridge and produces numerous small falls which accumulate together resulting in the Tangle Falls. In Winter the falls freeze over forming a wall of ice.* **(Below)**

Endless Chain Ridge *(Following page) Stretching 20 km along the Icefield Parkway the Endless Chain Ridge is a superb example of an overthrust mountain made of Gog quartzite.*

Sunwapta Falls (*Above*) *Cutting through the relatively soft limestone
at the Falls, the Sunwapta River is forced to make an abrupt 90 degree turn at the base of the
falls by the harder rock deposited by an ancient glacial moraine.*

Athabasca Falls (*Opposite*) *The Athabasca River feeds from the huge Athabasca glacier and
numerous other glaciers spilling from the Columbia and Chaba Icefields before forcing its
way through the narrow gorge at Athabasca Falls. The 25 meter falls are an impressive sight
from the many viewing points as they cut through some of the hardest rock in the region.*

JASPER
NATIONAL PARK

Encompassing 10,878 sq km Jasper is the largest park
in the Canadian Rockies. With a vertical rise
of 937m the Jasper Tramway provides a marvellous
opportunity to survey the landscape of
Jasper Town and the abundance of colorful lakes
that surround it. Looking north, the
Athabasca River can be seen flowing north to the Colin
Mountain Range, while Patricia and Pyramid
Lake can be seen to the west.

Jasper Town (*Opposite*) *The Whistler Mountain
Gondola offers a superb
panaramic view of the town and its surroundings.*

(*Previous page*) *Sunset over the Athabasca River.*

Angel Glacier (*Above*) *As ice melts at a higher rate than new ice is produced, Angle Glacier is retreating up the mountainside but still provides an excellent opportunity to view a hanging glacier close up.*

Mt Edith Cavell (*Opposite*) *at 3,363 m can be seen from a great distance. Known to natives as the "White Ghost," its unusual shape ensures that it is unmistakable. A road leads up to the foot of the mountain where it is possible to view its north face and hanging glacier. During the First World War the name "Edith Cavell" was given to this mountain to honour the heroism of a British nurse.*

Lac Beauvert (*Below*) with Mt. Edith Cavell clearly visible in the distance.

Pyramid Mountain (*Opposite*) shown here reflecting in Pyramid Lake, is
part of the Victoria Cross Mountain Range. The red rock is very hard sandstone which has turned
to quartz and is known as quartzite.

Patricia Lake (*Following page*) The area around Patricia Lake is one of the
best in Jasper Park for bird watching. Here a canada goose disturbs the mirror reflection
of the Trident Mountain range.

Trembling Aspen (*Below*) *is so named because the small leaves rustle in the breeze. It is easily identified by its silver/white bark. The leaves turn golden in the Autumn.*

Lake Edith *(Above) is one of over 40 fresh water lakes that surround Jasper town. It can be found at the beginning of the Maligne Lake road. On a calm clear day it is possible to see the reflection of Pyramid Mountain nestled on the other side of the town.*

Lake Annette *(Following page) An early morning mist drifts over the peaceful moonlit waters.*

Maligne Canyon From late Spring the Maligne River thunders 23 meters over the Maligne Falls *(below)*. During the Winter the water turns into ice columns with sheets of ice lining the canyon walls. Guides offer tours through the frozen narrow gorge in the Winter months *(opposite)*.

Maligne Lake *(Following page)* At over 22 km long and 97 m deep, Maligne Lake is the largest natural lake in the Canadian Rockies. Although it is glacier fed, its water appears less turquoise than some other lakes due to its size. However, the water is still vivid in color and Spirit Island offers a romantic location to view the lake as it stretches along the glacier studded peaks of the Elizabeth Mountain Range.

YOHO NATIONAL PARK

Yoho National Park, formerly called Mount Stephen Park, was established in 1885 and adjoins Banff Park to the west. The principal lake in the park is Emerald Lake which aptly describes the whole park. Although relatively small it is a valuable gem with a lot of stunning scenery within a small area. As the 'Cree' word implies, Yoho is a wonderful park. It has a protected upper subalpine region, a restricted area for Grizzly bears and a geological fossil site behind Mt. Burgess.

Abbot's Pass (Opposite) *provides mountaineers access to Lake O' Hara over Victoria Glacier from Lake Louise. Snow fall is possible at any time of the year at this altitude.*

Lake Ophutu (Following page) *is one of the numerous high mountain tarns which surround Lake O'Hara. The Lyall's Larch grows in abundance in this area and during the early Autumn the mountainside is ablaze as its needles turn golden yellow.*

*Lake O'Hara (**Opposite**) lies on the opposite side of Victoria Glacier at Lake Louise.*
To reduce the impact of tourism, there is limited access to this beautiful but fragile area except
for those prepared to hike. In restricting the number of visitors, the region offers a superb
example of a glacier landscape, rich with subalpine vegetation. With over 80 km
of trails leading to over 30 lakes, tundra plateaux, wildflower meadows and views like these, it
is easy to see why this is one of the most popular hiking areas in the Rockies.

Grizzly Bear (*Above*) To many people the most sensational wildlife sighting is a bear, and
the Canadian Rockies provide ample opportunity for bear sightings, particularly
along the quiet roads. A bear's natural instinct is to avoid humans which is why most
sightings are along the roadside rather than on back pack trails.
Approximately 200 grizzly bears roam the parks, but being more reclusive
than the opportunistic black bear, they prefer to stay in the higher alpine regions such as
Lake O'Hara, rather than coming down into the valleys.

*Lake O'Hara (**Following page**) At an elevation of over 2012 m, Lake O' Hara is*
one of the highest glacier lakes included in this book. Due to its elevation it remains snow
bound until July, leaving a very short Summer season for plant growth.

Spiral Tunnels *(Above) In 1909 underground loops were carved into the mountains, either side of the Kicking Horse Pass on the Continental Divide. The Spiral Tunnels were built to resolve the problem of runaway trains derailing as they sped down on the original line which ran from the Continental Divide to the town of Field. Named the "Big Hill," the original line had a 4.5% gradient which was twice that allowed under the Government legislation. The picture above shows both the front and rear end of a train as it enters and exits one of the tunnels.*

Takakkaw Falls *(Opposite) With a free fall of 254m the glacier fed Takakkaw Falls, or "Magnificent Falls," are one of the highest in Canada. The double drop enhances this impressive spectacle.*

The Natural Bridge *(Below) was once a waterfall. Over time the Kicking Horse River has cut its way down through its limestone bed. Debris and rock deposits have helped the water erode a new channel through the rock, widening the small cracks into an increasingly wider crevice which has left a bridge formation.*

Mt. Burgess *(Opposite) looms erect on the Eastern shores of Emerald Lake. After heavy snows and with a Winter temperature of -40° the scenery becomes a still and peaceful mono-color landscape.*

Emerald Lake (*Opposite*) *as its name suggests, is a
beautifully vivid and jewel-like example
of a glacier fed lake. The mountains to the north are part
of the President Range, and the dark forest helps to
enhance the emerald color. At an elevation of 1392m it is
one of the lower glacier fed lakes and is therefore
covered with ice for a shorter period of time.*

Calypso Orchid (*Above*) *A small and fragile early
blooming flower which
grows in the shade of the forest floor.*

MT ROBSON PROVINCIAL PARK

Bordering the western side of Jasper National Park,
Mount Robson Park provides a continuation
of spectacular scenery. Mount Robson itself, on a clear
day, is possibly the most breath-taking view
you will ever see in the Canadian Rockies. Hidden
from view until the last minute, the sudden
impact of seeing this massive mountain within very
close proximity to the actual road dramatises
its splendor. Its immense size and magnificence is
amplified all the more by the colossal drop
of glaciers and cliff walls on its north face. In the
words of the British explorer W.B. Cheadle;
"a giant amongst giants, and immeasureably supreme."

Mt Robson (*Opposite*) *is the highest peak in the
Canadian Rockies standing 3954 m tall. The SouthWest
face visible from the road rises a clear 3000 m,
which is a higher straight climb than any other mountain
in the Rockies of both Canada and America.*

Robson River (*Above*) *freezes over during
the Winter while the water
itself continues to flow several feet below the ice.*

Overland Falls (*Above*) *The Fraser River is a turbulent white water river. Flowing from glaciers along the Continental Divide it crashes over the Overland Falls near Mt Robson. The six meter falls become the end of the line for spawning salmon in early September.*

Mt Robson (*Opposite*) *Due to its immense size Mt Robson creates its own weather climate, and while there may be clear skies all around, the mountain often remains shrouded in cloud.*

KOOTENAY NATIONAL PARK

Like Banff National Park, it was the presence of the hot springs which led to
the establishment of Kootenay National Park in 1922. The Radium Hot Springs,
Marble Canyon and the Paint Pots, together with some excellent backpack
trails, are the main attractions to the park. The relatively small number of visitors to the
park make it ideal for viewing wildlife.

Mt. Verendrye (*Above*) *3093 m high is one of the highest peaks of the Rockwall Mountain
Range which is a popular area for hikers.*

Marble Canyon (*Opposite*) *is one of the deepest canyons in
the Rockies, at 36 m deep. A good trail offers numerous vantage points to view the
Tokumm Creek thundering over falls through the canyon.*

Paint Pots (*Above*) *So called because the earth in this area has been
stained red with iron oxide, which comes from underground springs that form red pools of
water. Kutenai Natives used the colored clay for body paint.*

Sinclair Canyon (*Opposite*) *The present road running through Sinclair Canyon replaces the
original road which was washed away. The creek which
runs through the canyon now flows underneath the road. The Radium Hot Springs permeate
on the other side of the canyon.*

GLACIER NATIONAL PARK

Roger's Pass Summit *(Above) is 1330m above sea level and provides an excellent opportunity to see a few of the 422 glaciers in the park. Good trails offer backpackers a chance to view some of the other glaciers.*

Bighorn Sheep *(Above) Fairly common throughout the parks the rams grow up to three feet in height. Although both male and female have horns, which are not shed each year, the rams' horns are much larger, as shown above.*